TEACHING KIDS ABOUT MONEY

5 SIMPLE STRATEGIES FOR PARENTS TO EQUIP KIDS WITH FINANCIAL LITERACY FROM TODDLER TO TEEN YEARS

REESE FRAZIER

SAGE

ISBN: 978-1-958118-03-0

TRILLIUM SAGE PUBLISHING | WWW.TRILLIUMSAGE.COM

3943 IRVINE BLVD #138, IRVINE, CA 92602

To my three monkeys...
Kieran, Kendall, and Brennan

...thank you for inspiring me
(to read more parenting books).

Do not save what is left after spending, but spend what is left after saving.

- Warren Buffet

CONTENTS

INTRODUCTION

Starting from the time when they were barely able to identify shapes and colors correctly, I started teaching my sons about money. I did this to prepare them for when they were ready to fly the nest some fifteen short years later. Fifteen years go by in a snap, and in addition to money management, there were so many other essential life lessons to bestow upon them while they were still under my roof. When my husband passed away unexpectedly, my eldest son was only in middle school, which further motivated me to teach them as much as I knew.

As I witnessed so many friends in college fall victim to snowballing credit card debt, I was fueled with the desire to make sure my kids were given a proper foundation regarding personal finance and have a healthy relationship with money. This book aims to create the framework from the early years for kids to have a natural habit of treating money responsibly once they are out in the real world. This framework is critical to the success they will achieve as adults.

I hope this book will help you think creatively about setting up your kids' view of money and making responsible spending habits second nature. My aim is not for our children to become obsessed with money, but rather to have a healthy relationship with it to make good decisions later on. As they learn to respect money, they will come to see it as a means to do more for others and themselves.

ONE

GROUND RULES

Growing up, my parents constantly stressed education as the top priority and did not encourage me to work while I was in high school. They felt that this allowed me to concentrate on my studies fully. However, as I see it now, this turned out to be a missed opportunity. This did not teach me to handle money as an adult responsibly. Additionally, because I always felt like I was asking for money, I would feel guilty whenever I *did* ask. It's not quite the same going out with friends having this over my head. My parents never stressed chores either, which made me lazy and a disaster for a college roommate! Learning from my childhood experience, I knew I wanted to teach my kids a different approach.

I would never claim to be a financial guru. I'm just a mom who only wants the best for her kids. Simple as that. The ideas and concepts presented here are meant to be fun and practical as they set up kids for their future financial success. I'm going to keep it as simple, manageable, and fun for parents as it is for kids so that it holds everyone's interest and commitment for the long term. Some topics might seem very surface-level, but they are just a starting point for you to investigate further on your own to see how they might fit into your financial environment.

I used the amount of money that was comfortable for me within my budgetary constraints to teach my three sons Kieran, Kendall, and Brennan. Please feel free to increase or decrease the amounts suggested in this book to fit your unique financial situation.

Suppose your kids receive any money from other sources within your family (grandparents, aunts, uncles, etc.). In that case, I highly recommend that you have a delicate conversation with them about your intention as you teach your kids. I didn't want my kids wondering, "Why should I work so hard when I can just get free money from my grandparents?!" The structure of building a foundation in the toddler years and at each subsequent year or stage is for parents to determine when their child is ready to add another layer to the existing layer. Like not being able to run until they can walk, we will plan on teaching baby steps so that the next level is not daunting or too much of a challenge. Of course, it is ideal to start when our kids are young.

However, any time you can implement these habits is beneficial.

At each level of their childhood, we will cover the following five areas in various capacities:

- Chores: Teaching responsibility and helping others
- Income: Earning through work
- Money Management: Financial responsibility
- Entertainment: Fun ways to learn with money
- Education: Continual process of adding to their financial knowledge

Alright, now that everyone's on the same page, let's get started!

TWO

THE TODDLER YEARS

Ah, the toddler years...This was such a fun age! So much growth happens in this three to four-year-old range. They are past their terrible twos, and even though they've now graduated to their treacherous threes, I found that they were more reasonable than before. Well, at least two of my three kids were! To keep things simple, we're going to start easy with just three goals.

Goals:

- Introduce the concept of helping around the house (chores)
- Introduce currency (income)
- Introduce money management (save, donate, spend)

CHORES

When my eldest son, Kieran, turned three, my husband and I agreed it was the right time to talk to him about finance. We sat Kieran down and explained that we have something exciting we're going to start doing. Be sure to make a big deal of this, as your excitement will set the stage. In fact, at this age, anything with fanfare is generally greeted with much enthusiasm! We announced that now that he was a big boy at three years old, we will expect Kieran to help out around the house.

The list of chores we wanted Kieran to complete was simple and could include any of the listed tasks below (at any stage, please feel free to assign duties to your kids as much as you think they can potentially do an excellent job). Only set as many as you think will be comfortable for your child to be challenged but not overwhelmed.

- Put toys and books where they belong
- Put away folded laundry
- Place dirty clothes in the hamper
- Dust
- Sweep
- Make their bed
- Clean up any minor spills or messes they make

INCOME

My husband and I next explained that since he was responsible enough now to do chores like us, for his hard work, he would be rewarded with our home currency, "Benjamins" (named after my husband). We had paper money printed on green cardstock in different denominations, complete with a ridiculous picture of my husband in the center. You can easily purchase fake money to use, as well.

We explained that every Friday was payday, and if he did his chores all week, as we discussed, he would earn three Benjamins. Three whole Benjamins! For simple math, each Benjamin was worth one dollar.

MONEY MANAGEMENT

We introduced money management by explaining to Kieran that his money would be sorted into three separate categories: save, donate, and spend. We then went into more detail and explained what each of the categories meant. For "save," this simply meant money that we put aside and pretend that it's not there. It's an emergency fund and not to be used unless absolutely necessary. I seriously can't think of what a financial emergency might look like for a three-year-old, but the concept is what we're teaching here! We're building that foundation.

Next, we discussed "donate." I want to teach my boys to think of others and to help them out when they can. Again, this is another fund that we only tap into when there is a valid need. At this age, donation simply meant offering for church.

Lastly, we talked about "spend." This was the most fun category to explain! We told Kieran that he could use his "spend" Benjamins to buy things when we're out and about because he already saved and donated.

We also made a rule that once Benjamins went into the jar, they were not to be transferred to a different jar. This was a deterrent from moving money around to suit other needs conveniently.

ENTERTAINMENT

On Kieran's first payday, we made a big deal of it and thanked him for his hard work and handed him three crisp Benjamins. I prepared three jars, each with a picture depicting the three categories of "save, donate, and spend" since Kieran could not read yet. My kids were visual learners, so it made a far more significant positive impact on seeing their jars fill up as they earned more. Kids are simple, and Kieran's eyes lit up as he stuffed his first Benjamins in each jar. There was a lot of satisfaction in adding to the existing Benjamins in the jars and watching them fill up.

. . .

EDUCATION

When you feel like your child is ready to handle real money, you can convert his home currency to real, cold hard cash. Each time I was to leave the house to shop, I converted Kieran's Benjamins into actual currency. I placed his money in an envelope with "Bank" written on the front and served as the bank to hold onto his cash until he wanted to spend it. This saved many a meltdown in the toy aisle, as we came to learn.

Whenever Kieran wanted to buy something, I'd first respond with, "Let's see how much we have in the bank." We would then count out how much money he had in the bank and if he had enough to make the purchase, great! If not, I would explain that he simply did not have enough money...yet. I didn't give him a hard "no." I wanted him to work on saving towards a goal. This was also a perfect opportunity to explain that he simply can't spend what he doesn't have.

THREE

THE ELEMENTARY SCHOOL YEARS

So now that our ex-toddlers are entering their elementary school careers, we're going to step it up a level. With each level up, they are given more responsibility in their chores, the potential to earn more income, and more privileges. Goals for this five to ten-year-old range are just a tad bit more than what they are used to from before.

Goals:

- Introduction of real cash
- Allowance based on the quality of chores
- Opening a savings account
- Being generous to others

CHORES

There is a much greater ability, at this age, to take on more responsibility. Appropriate chores for elementary school-aged kids may include the following, in addition to duties already taught:

- unload the dishwasher
- take out trash and recycles to the bins
- bring in the mail
- feed, walk, clean up after the dog (or general care for another pet)
- set the table for meals
- tidy up common areas
- refill napkins on the dinner table
- bring in and put away groceries
- wash and fold laundry
- change bed sheets
- water plants
- sweep
- rake the yard

If you have more than one child, be sure to rotate chores between them based on their age, maturity, and physical ability, so that everyone knows how to handle each household responsibility. This occurred to me when my boys only had their usual chores. I asked one of the boys to do a simple task that his brother usually did, and he had NO idea how!

So, from that time on, I rotated chores between them every quarter.

INCOME

When my boys were five years old, we allowed them to earn real money. By now, they were accustomed to the "save, donate, spend" model and were ready to turn in their Benjamins for actual currency. Their age determined their income. The boys now had the *potential* to earn $1 for each year of their age per week. For example, at five years old, they can make up to $5 a week. However, this $5 a week was not guaranteed.

Now that they were a bit older, we explained that their income is based on their chore output quality that week. I wanted my sons to understand that money is not *given*, but rather, it is *earned*.

If they did not receive their total amount that week, it allowed me to explain why and for them to work to meet expectations the following week. If they forgot to do their chores, did a sub-par job, or had to be reminded to do their tasks, their income would be affected negatively. I expected my sons to strive for excellence, not perfection. If I can see that they honestly performed to the best of their ability, they earned their full income that week.

· · ·

MONEY MANAGEMENT

We built on what was taught in the toddler years with money management. Still following the "save, donate, spend" model, we added a new layer. From this point on, whatever amount my boys decided to save would be matched for their "save" funds. Much like how some companies match 401k contributions in the workplace, we would match dollar for dollar. The more they contributed, the more they would save over time.

When each of my boys turned five years old, I would take him to the bank to open a savings account. This was quite a big deal to my kids! They loved seeing their name on anything official.

I explained that as they saved their money, it would be kept here at the bank until later. Be sure to check with your banking institution as to what necessary documents are required to open a savings account for a minor. Often, it's a parent's driver's license and documentation for the child (Social Security card, birth certificate, immunization record, school ID, or passport).

We also continued to encourage our kids to contribute regularly to their "donate" jar. My kids enjoyed being able to help people out and donated to causes that touched them.

In addition to using their donations for church offering, they now also used their money to donate to worthy causes such as:

- charities (e.g., World Vision)
- fundraising campaigns for natural disaster relief (e.g., Samaritan's Purse)
- grief camps for bereaved children (e.g., Experience Camps)
- any general community needs that moved them

It brought me such joy to hear, "Mama, how much money do I have in my donation fund?"

Years ago, we attended a concert, and there was a campaign to sponsor a child who was in desperate need of life's basic necessities. My then seven-year-old son, Brennan, shocked to hear that children didn't even have clean water to drink, turned to me and asked if we could sponsor a child. I was thrilled that he recognized another child's needs and wanted to help, so I gladly agreed to it.

I believe it is up to us as parents to teach our kids about social responsibility. In doing so, our kids learn empathy. Kids will naturally think of themselves first, so we should encourage them to think outwardly whenever possible. One of the ways we can do this is to present opportunities to help others.

There are plenty of occasions to encourage kids to help others who are not as fortunate as they are. This can be done in different ways with their time (volunteering) or money (donations).

Each Christmas, I share the World Vision catalog with my boys and ask if they would like to buy any animals for families in need from around the world. They read stories about families who, in one example, would benefit from owning and raising farm animals to sell eggs or milk as a source of income. They also learned that to prevent disease, families needed mosquito nets to protect them as they slept.

If they felt led, they would let me know, and we would purchase something from the catalog. Knowing that they were helping others with their actions allowed them to think of other ways to use their donation funds.

The "spend" fund was again the fun reward for their hard work. This could be spent on what kids want, but parents still have an ultimate say in the matter. I do encourage parents to be a bit more lenient here with how kids spend their money. It's meant for them to have fun with it. They rightfully earned this money through their efforts.

As long as it was not something harmful to them or others (or illegal!), I leaned more towards "yes" rather than "no." It was difficult, but I would bite my tongue when they wanted to spend their hard-earned money on some, in my opinion, straight-up dumb purchase.

I hoped that as they made these frivolous purchases, the short-lived fun of the splurge might deter them from doing the same next time. But once again, this was money that they earned and should be allowed to spend as they wish.

We want to get kids into the mindset that they can afford to treat themselves to a bit of fun after they worked hard for it and after they have already put a portion of their earnings aside for savings and donations.

ENTERTAINMENT

The elementary years were fun to teach about finances. Some fun things we did:

- When we ate out, we told the kids that if they wanted to get a soda or any other special drink, they would have to pay for it themselves. However, if they opted for water or milk, they'd get a dollar. This allowed the boys to consider their decision and whether something was worth the cost.
- These elementary years between my three boys proved to be prime time for losing teeth and Tooth Fairy visits. For some time there, it felt like the Tooth Fairy was at our house every week! Instead of just sneaking them a dollar for each tooth, I explained to my kids that they had to write the Tooth Fairy a letter describing how they lost their tooth for her to visit. I also told the boys that if their rooms were messy, the Tooth Fairy was less apt to visit them.
- I never liked having loose change jingling in my pocket. I hardly use cash, but in the rare moments

when I do and am given change, I would let one of
the boys count out the loose change, and if he were
correct, he got to keep it.

- My boys were never academically driven, so to
encourage them to read, I would pay a dollar per
one-page book report for each book they read. The
reports didn't have to be lengthy, but just a fun
way to motivate them to read more. You can easily
find printable one-page book report forms online.

- The boys' grandparents offered to pay hefty
bonuses for straight-A report cards. Though this
bounty has existed for years, my parents have not
had to depart with their money!

EDUCATION

The elementary years presented numerous opportunities to
teach many lessons. From taxes to responsibility to making
good choices, money was a good way for my boys to process
information and make decisions.

We spent a fair bit of time at the local toy shop in town
during these years. My boys loved just to visit the store to see
what they might be able to save up for next.

One lesson learned during this time was the existence of
sales tax. When my boys thought they had enough money to
make a purchase, they happily announced that they wanted
to visit the toy store. When the item rang up at the cash
register, they were shocked and disappointed to learn that

the toy they thought they could afford would cost a bit more than anticipated. They failed to factor sales tax into the equation.

The kind store owner explained that this happened all the time. He even had a jar on the counter for kids to borrow from to pay the tax. I wasn't too keen on this as I was adamant about teaching my boys that they can't buy anything if they didn't already have the money in hand, but the store owner convinced me just to let it slide this once. I made a note of how much my son borrowed, and as soon as he earned enough to repay the store owner, we made a trip back to the store to do so.

This season was also an excellent time to teach responsibility. If the boys broke anything, it was his responsibility to make it right.

When Brennan was in elementary school, he slammed the door to the garage open in a fit of boiling rage. The door stop proved no match for the fury of a disgruntled six-year-old. From Brennan's actions, the doorknob created a 3-inch hole in the wall. I explained to him that we take care of our property, and to fix the hole in the wall, he was financially responsible for the handyman's time and effort.

My handyman created an invoice and handed it to Brennan - $50! Brennan's eyes looked like they were going to pop out of his head because he understood how long it would take him to pay me back for his mistake. His "spend" money went directly towards paying down his costly $50 mistake for many weeks. He was much more careful with how he treated our home and property after that painful lesson!

Not to use money as a weapon, but it can powerfully help influence kids' decisions. During his elementary school years, Kieran started "being sick" a lot and often asked to stay home. To deter these sick days, I told Kieran that the next time he was "sick," we would make a trip to the urgent care center. If the doctor determined that he was indeed sick, I would willingly cover the $25 co-pay.

However, if, after the examination, the doctor thinks Kieran was in good health and should be at school, Kieran would have to cover the co-pay. Soon after the implementation of this rule, Kieran miraculously had a string of perfectly healthy days. Imagine that!

FOUR

THE MIDDLE SCHOOL YEARS

As my sweet elementary school-aged boys entered their smelly angst-ridden middle school years, I continued to alter their financial education to fit their needs. Another layer added to chores, income, money management, entertainment, and education. Since they have been doing this for years, both my expectations and theirs all seemed pretty manageable. We included new goals for this eleven to thirteen-year-old range.

Goals:

- Opening a teen account at the bank
- Opening an investment account
- Learning to take initiative
- Learning about delayed gratification

CHORES

A great way to burn off some of that middle school energy is by introducing more chores to the boys' existing chore repertoire. Kids develop at different rates, so try to assign duties that you know your kids can do well yet challenge them. In addition to what they have already learned and likely mastered, I also added the following:

- clean bathroom (toilet, counters, mirrors, floors, shower, tub, empty trash)
- vacuum
- wipe down the dining table
- wipe down kitchen counters
- take trash and recycle bins to the curb
- load the dishwasher
- clean the porch
- clean the backyard
- pack healthy lunch and snacks for school
- wash windows
- prepare light meals
- babysit younger siblings

INCOME

There are not too many changes in this area during this phase of childhood. My boys continued to earn as many dollars per week as their age potentially. In addition to their income, however, I introduced another way to make more per week if they were interested.

There were several jobs at home that I was either too busy or tired to do on my own as a single mom, so I outsourced them to my kids. I had a running list of such projects on my phone's "to do" list, each accompanied with the dollar value of how much I was willing to pay to have the task completed. These were minor projects that were easy to complete as time allowed and weren't more than a few bucks here and there. This was a win-win as I saw it.

The job board provided me a way to retain my sanity and efficiency while giving the boys a quick income source if they decided to take the initiative.

Again, as with their chores, I expected their best efforts, and they would only be paid if I was satisfied by the quality of the work they did.

Such projects were done on a sporadic basis (unlike daily chores) and could include such projects as:

- clean out the fridge
- clean out the garage
- organize the garage
- reorganize the pantry
- touch up paint on walls
- clean the ceiling fans
- clean shutters and windowsills

Money Management

As the kids were a bit older now, I challenged them to adjust the proportions of the save, donate, spend model to put aside at least 20% for saving and 20% for donation. This still allowed them 60% to spend. If they monitored their savings accounts and watched how quickly their savings grew because of the one-to-one matching, they might be inclined to save more than just 20%. I continued to emphasize that as they are blessed, they should also bless others in the form of donations.

When my kids turned 13, they became eligible to open teen accounts at our local bank. This was the official place to hold their spending money.

One of the perks of this account was that my sons now had a debit card, which allowed them to make purchases on their own when they shopped online or met up with friends. It was also very convenient for me to transfer their spending and savings from income into their bank accounts.

It was interesting to see how my kids managed their money now that they were a bit older. If they wanted to attend a friend's party, they were responsible for buying a gift for their friend. This helped them decide how to spend both their time and their money.

ENTERTAINMENT

The middle school age range is when I felt comfortable with my sons earning money from other sources. Kieran, who was quite the entrepreneur, ran a few successful businesses at this age. He offered his services to help dog sit for neighbors as well.

When the boys were younger, I hired my friend's eighth-grade daughter as a "mother's helper" to assist with the kids just so that I was able to cook in peace. She would come over in the afternoon a couple of times a week to play with the boys, do crafts, help with homework...basically anything just as long as they didn't interrupt me in the kitchen! It was fun for her and the boys, and it gave me a break as a weary mom.

It is advisable for kids at this age to ask trusted family, friends, and neighbors if they need help with anything. Some simple, informal starter jobs might include:

- tutor elementary school kids
- be a mother's helper
- wash cars
- dog walking
- dog sitting
- rent out their toys or books
- make and sell things (e.g., jewelry, cookies, etc.)
- sell unwanted items from around the house (with parental permission!)

- recycle items
- teach younger kids how to play video games
- babysit

EDUCATION

Kids are naturally impulsive, and in today's fast-paced world, with next-day shipping and constant social media updates, it is effortless to be sucked into a world of instant gratification. I make every attempt to help my boys with this. If they wanted to buy something, especially a big-ticket item, I would suggest that they sit on the idea for seven days. If, at the end of the week, they still want to buy it, they can. But repeatedly, as I've witnessed, they change their minds. I also encouraged them to set up separate savings funds (from their "spend" money) to save for items they want to buy.

The central part of education at this age was my boys' introduction to investing. I kept it as simple as possible, nothing fancy, as they just started to learn. We'll build more upon this topic in the high school years. The money they have been saving all these years has been sitting in their savings account at the bank. Now that they were a bit older, I wanted to tell them about a better way to grow their savings in investing.

I opened custodial accounts through a brokerage firm for my kids when they were in middle school. I used the money that they've been saving up all these years to open their accounts. Custodial accounts, also known as Uniform Gifts to Minors Act (UGMA) accounts or Uniform Transfers to Minors Act (UTMA) accounts, are a simple first step to get kids thinking about investing. Some brief notes about custodial accounts:

- You manage the account, but the account is created and held in your child's name.
- The custodial account must be handed over to your child when they reach 18, 21, or 25 (depending on your state). At this time, you will surrender any control of the account over to your child, and they are free to do with it as they wish.
- When applying for financial aid in college, 20% of the assets will be taken into calculations.

There are benefits and drawbacks regarding taxes (e.g., gift tax, kiddie tax, etc.) with custodial accounts. For more detailed information, please consult your tax professional or your brokerage firm.

I talked to my boys about the stock market, and if they would like, they could purchase tiny parts of the companies they are familiar with in the name of shares. Of course, my boys couldn't afford many shares because of their accounts' limited balances. Thankfully, their custodial accounts are with a brokerage that allows for the purchase of fractional shares of S&P 500 companies. So even though they weren't able to purchase a whole share of a company, if it was listed in the S&P 500, they could own just a teeny, tiny bit of it.

We used Schwab Stock Slices for this. I encouraged them to think about companies that they liked, but to be on the safer side, most of their positions are with companies in the S&P 500.

Growing up in these times, my boys leaned heavily into the technology sector and purchased most of their stocks in this area. I advised that it would probably be a good idea to diversify their portfolio by including other industries. Because of their small account size, the best way to diversify at this time was through ETFs (exchange-traded funds). This allowed for diversification within their limited assets.

I also let my sons know that companies pay dividends to shareholders every once in a while, and they can reinvest their dividends to get more shares. As a general rule, I explained that we're not going to be moving money around the stock market for their goals. We will instead be buying, holding, and riding out any bumps. I also encouraged them to keep some of their money in cash so that if there were to be a dip in the market, they would be able to buy stocks "on sale."

When the boys were given money for their birthdays or Christmas, they would put a portion into their investments (knowing that I'd match). They will then let me know if they want to add more shares to existing positions or purchase new stocks. It has been fun teaching them about stocks and showing them how their accounts have grown over time. Had their money continued sitting in their savings accounts, they would not have enjoyed these gains.

If your child is responsible enough and can be trusted with social media, I recommend following some finance people on Instagram. There are numerous people to follow, but my favorites, @CarbonFinance, @FinanceJosh, and @TheInvestorDad, put out some of the most informative and visually appealing finance content. Kids will likely understand the simple infographics that are posted.

More importantly, seeing these posts in your child's feed daily is an easy way to keep them thinking and growing in their financial literacy.

I told the boys that their investments would continue to grow over time as they invest in their accounts. When they graduate high school and leave home, I will give the account to them, and it will be up to them, at that point, how they want to use the money. They may use it for college expenses, a trip, or (my hope!) furthering their investments.

FIVE

THE HIGH SCHOOL YEARS

And just like that, in a flash, your kids are in high school! These mini-adults are well on their way to being financially responsible. They have the basics down, and we are now going to focus on their future. These are lessons that they can put into action during and after high school. It is crucial that as kids learn and possibly make mistakes, they do so while still at home and under our guidance. As parents, we act as their invisible safety net and coach them through any potential missteps.

Goals:

- getting a job
- creating and living within a budget
- discussing long-term financial goals
- expanding financial knowledge

CHORES

At this high school level, they have mastered all the chores in previous years and will have the ability to do the following (and whatever else parents think their kids are capable of doing!):

- wash the car
- steam clean floors and carpet
- grocery shop
- plan budget for meals
- cook
- organize their closet
- iron clothes
- run errands

When kids are in high school, they will have many more time commitments than in their younger years. Whether it be spending more time studying, practicing sports, working at an after-school job, volunteering, or hanging with friends, it is still essential that high schoolers continue contributing to household responsibilities. In his high school years, I vaguely recall Kieran offering to pay off his younger brother, Kendall, to do some of his chores simply because he lacked time!

INCOME

High schoolers will most likely have a greater desire for more money between increased social commitments and higher-priced material goods as their spending needs also grow. To supplement what they receive at home for their household contributions, they should also get a job to afford their new lifestyle. I have always encouraged my kids to find their first jobs in the service industry as I firmly believe serving others will help give them a greater appreciation when they are on the other side of the transaction. I would recommend looking first at establishments that line up with your teen's interests. Some places and roles for first jobs:

- busboy
- cashier
- coffee shop
- concessions
- golf course
- grocery stores
- ice cream shop
- lifeguard
- restaurant host/hostess
- retail stores
- waiter
- yardwork

If your child has an entrepreneurial spirit, he or she might want to consider starting their own business in their expertise. Teens can be super creative with this! Parents of other children (especially young children) are often willing to pay for instruction by responsible teens as it would be much more cost-effective than learning from a professional. Some areas to consider include:

- dance instructor
- hiking guide
- physical trainer
- skateboard instructor
- snowboard instructor
- swim instructor
- trainer for youth sports
- tutor

MONEY MANAGEMENT

We will continue to stress the "save, donate, and spend" model of money management. By now, teens will be very familiar with this model and may readjust the proportions according to their needs.

Allow them to have more freedom and independence now that they are a bit older. There should still be an emphasis on saving and donating as these are the areas that will take more discipline. However, it may not take much effort as they are already accustomed to this practice.

We will introduce setting and staying within a budget at this age. Kids need to grasp the concept that they have to stay within their income and budget their money accordingly to not run into debt. Creating a simple spreadsheet, such as the one below, will help monitor their spending. You will find fancier templates online if you prefer. Of course, you may edit the categories listed to fit your teen's individual spending requirements.

Category	Budgeted	Actual					
		January	February	March	April	May	June
Clothes							
Emergency Savings Fund							
Food							
Fuel							
Gifts							
Investment							
Special Savings Fund							
Spending							
Subscriptions							
Travel							

At the beginning of each month, your teen should input how much they spent in these categories for the previous month. They will then compare it to how much they had budgeted. Suppose they are over budget consistently in one particular category over some time. In that case, they might consider increasing that budget (while decreasing another category to make up for it), working on spending less in that category, or both of the above.

I do advise two funds outside of the usual savings categories: Emergency Savings Fund and Special Savings Fund. These two funds are outside of what is for their savings/investment account. Emergency Savings is just to set aside a small amount monthly for unexpected expenses. Special Savings is for creating a fund to make special big-ticket purchases in the future.

ENTERTAINMENT

As teens mature and earn their own money, there are more opportunities to have fun learning about money. They now have the freedom to spend as they please, within their budget limits.

A few years ago, I took my three boys out to dinner on my birthday. When the bill came, I reached for the check, and Kieran, now in his freshman year in high school, asked me how much dinner cost. I thought it was interesting that he should care because he's never asked before. He then asked if it was less than $50. When I quizzically nodded that it was, his eyes lit up, and he proudly announced, "Awesome, because your birthday dinner is on me!" I was shocked that he offered to buy dinner for our family but was so touched that he did. Seeing him spend his money on me instead of putting it towards his savings goal for a new snowboard was just an incredible moment for me as a mom, and I was sure to express my appreciation. I could tell from Kieran's smile that he was happy to do this for me as well.

As my kids continued to save and grow their investments, I began to teach them more about investing. I enrolled them in a few online courses to learn the basics of investing and how to trade stocks. I also started them on a paper trading account to practice what they learned. This was an excellent way for them to test their strategies and see how they might grow their fake investment accounts.

It cost nothing to them if they made mistakes, allowed them to learn from their mistakes, and prepared them for when they were old enough to manage their investment accounts with real money. Remember, at age 18 (or whatever age is deemed by your state), the custodial account you have been managing will be transferred to your child. You want to ensure that they will have the knowledge and experience to manage their account responsibly as they continue to invest.

EDUCATION

While we have our kids at home in this last stage of their childhood, we must take full advantage to educate them as much as possible.

Reading books is one common habit shared by the world's famous billionaires. Warren Buffet, Elon Musk, and Bill Gates are all known to be voracious readers.

I encourage my kids to read as this could very well correlate to their financial success later on in life. The more knowledge they attain now, the better. A few of the books on my kids' high school reading list include:

- *7 Habits of Highly Effective Teens* by Sean Covey

- *Rich Dad Poor Dad for Teens* by Robert T. Kiyosaki
- *The Early Investor* by Michael Zisa
- *I Want More Pizza* by Steve Burkholder
- *What You Should've Learned About Money, But Never Did* by Sophia Bera

When my kids are around successful people, I encourage them to talk to them and ask them just one question. Over time, the answers to their questions accumulate and broaden their knowledge of what it takes for success.

Questions such as "How do you push through challenges?", "What is one thing you did that impacted your success?" or "If you had to start over, what is one thing you would do differently?" are thought-provoking and great conversation starters. Of course, I only encourage my kids to start these conversations when appropriate, natural, and not annoying to others.

Kieran recently shared that when he was on a ski lift with his uncle, he simply listened to a conversation between his uncle and a friend, and even in that short amount of time, he was able to gain some knowledge of the business world. Our kids must make the most of the opportunities they have exposure to because it's all part of their education. Had Kieran done the typical teen thing and blasted music through his headphones on that ski lift, he would have missed out on an opportunity to learn and grow.

Even though it is decades into the future, I like to discuss long-term financial goals with my kids when they're in high school. Retirement seems a lifetime from now, and it pretty much is at this age, but with time on their side, it is only to their advantage to begin thinking and planning.

Even before they start their careers, high school kids can open a Roth IRA. As they deposit a small portion of the money they earn from their jobs, they will enjoy tax-free benefits as their investments grow over time. Here's a brief rundown of a Roth IRA account (once again, please consult a professional for more details):

- maximum earned contribution of $6,000 annually (since teens are less than 50 years old)
- contributions are withdrawn tax-free
- withdrawing earnings may be taxed

A short 10-year delay in starting such an account can make a tremendous difference in the outcome. In 2018, Fidelity Investments calculated the following based on a 7% rate of return and the maximum annual earnings (at the time, in 2018) of $5,500 contributed into a Roth IRA:

- at age 65, the account would have grown to $2.4 million if started at age 15
- at age 65, the account would have grown to $1.2 million if started at age 25

Much of this is due to compounding, which might not sound all that exciting to a high schooler! However, when you explain that they are earning on top of what they have already earned (basically "free money"), and their account grows faster because of this, they might be intrigued.

Another topic of discussion I like to have with my kids is about having multiple streams of income. Outside of their eventual careers, I recommend them to secure other means to generate revenue. This will provide stability in the off-chance that they suddenly lose their jobs due to unforeseen circumstances. Some simple ways to supplement their 9-5 jobs can include:

- side hustles: freelance writing, driving services, blogging
- rental income: renting out property or cars you own and don't regularly use
- trading in the stock market
- dividend investing
- flipping retail products

Towards the end of high school, our kids are pretty much adults. Even with all that you've already taught them, there is always room to grow their financial literacy. There are many facets to financial literacy. Having the proper mindset and foundation, as you have created all these years, will keep our kids wanting to learn more about securing their finances for the future.

SIX

KIERAN THE ENTREPRENEUR: A CASE STUDY

I want to encourage parents to support their kids in even the most minor ways as they start to learn about money. Kieran has always had an entrepreneurial mindset, and from a very young age, the tiny money-making gears in his head were spinning.

When Kieran was in fifth grade, rubber band bracelets were all the rage. He approached me and asked if I would be interested in investing in his business by contributing a little money towards his start-up costs.

I asked Kieran to tell me about his business. He said that he sees all the kids at school wearing these rubber band bracelets. He wanted to make a bunch of bracelets during the weekend and sell them to his classmates.

I decided to support him and his business, and I agreed to take him to the craft store to purchase some of the initial materials. He spent his weekend making bracelets and on Monday, went to school and sold them to friends. He sold many bracelets but observed that everyone pretty much made and wore all the same kinds of bracelets. They could easily create their own bracelets and might not necessarily be interested in purchasing his.

Kieran came home and told me that he was going to do something different. Instead of making bracelets, the same kind all the kids at school had, he spent the weekend watching videos online on creating far more elaborate bracelets. Additionally, Kieran also reinvested his initial profits into the business and purchased hard-to-find metal-lic-looking rubber bands online. Kieran did not have to advertise because when he went to school wearing his new bracelet, a design other kids had never seen before, they were excited and interested.

He received many orders for these more elaborate bracelets. Kieran also decided to give his friends $1 in commission for each bracelet they helped to sell. His first business was a success, and he was hooked!

The following year in middle school, Kieran launched a few more small businesses. With some of the money he received for his birthday, he purchased a box of 25 speed cubes. The package cost him roughly $25, essentially $1/cube. Kieran could flip these pocket-sized toys for $3/cube to his classmates, making a sweet profit of $2/cube. When I asked him why his classmates bought them from him instead of just getting them online themselves, Kieran explained that he could get them cheaper than if he were to purchase them individually because he was buying so many cubes. Most kids his age either didn't have the money to buy it themselves or didn't want to make such a high-volume purchase. It was fascinating to me to watch his young business mind at work!

Another year goes by, and Kieran has another business idea. He started to hear about fidget spinners and their quick rise in popularity. He learned to make his fidget spinners with skateboard bearings and zip ties and began selling them to friends. Kieran customized his spinners based on requests from friends and in their favorite color combinations.

Once Kieran was in high school, he was busier than before, with academics taking up more of his time, but that did not stop him from exploring new business ideas. He was always on the lookout to see what he could sell.

When Kieran was congested one day, I gave him an inhaler I got from the pharmacy that contained different essential oils to help him breathe. It worked so well for him that he asked me what other essential oils might help other symptoms. I explained that essential oils are used for various purposes, and he decided to read more about them. Kieran figured what would help his friends at school the most and created a line of essential oil inhalers to help alleviate stress, give sinus relief, help with focus in class, and energize.

With a bit more business experience under his belt, he put more effort towards creating a product with an aesthetically pleasing label and chose colors based on how they might affect someone psychologically. Once again, he used his vast network of friends to help market his products.

It was fun to watch Kieran's business mind evolve through the years. He learned many aspects about being an entrepreneur from these start-ups, all while making a little cash on the side. If you have an entrepreneur in your home, feed their curiosity and support them however you can because it just might lead to bigger things down the road.

FINAL WORDS

We covered a lot of ground here teaching our kids about money - from their toddler years to their high school years (and beyond!). My goal is to teach our kids to continue to manage money as it has been introduced to them as they grew up in our home. Good habits formed over the years should continue in their young careers. As they start their own families, these habits will prioritize how they manage their money. With finances being a prevalent and sensitive topic in relationships, all they have learned and implemented through these years should serve them well.

When it boils down to it, the message is simply for our kids to work hard, play hard, bless others, manage money wisely, and always strive to continue learning. Having more money is a mighty force. It will amplify the good or bad - if kids were generous before, they would give more. However, if they were irresponsible before, they will be even more so. As our kids continue to treat money as we have taught them, they will enjoy much success in their financial future!

SPECIAL REQUEST

WANT TO HELP OTHER PARENTS SET UP THEIR KIDS WITH FUTURE FINANCIAL SUCCESS?

If you have enjoyed *Teaching Kids About Money*, I would be incredibly thankful if you would take just 60 seconds to leave a brief review wherever you purchased this book - even if it's just a few sentences.

Thank you!

https://tinyurl.com/ 2p8a63kp

RESOURCES

Aguirre, S. A. (2020, October 9). *Age-Appropriate Chores for Kids Ages 2 to 18*. Thespruce.Com. https://www.thespruce.com/age-appropriate-chore-charts-1900357

Albert, M. A. (2014, November 25). *The Best Nonfiction Books for Teens*. Barnesandnoble.Com. https://www.barnesandnoble.com/blog/the-best-nonfiction-books-for-teens/

Angryelf, A. (2021, February 26). *11 Ways 12-, 13-, or 14-Year-Old Middle School Kids Can Earn Money*. Wehavekids.Com. https://wehavekids.com/parenting/10-Ways-A-12-13-or-14-Year-Old-Can-Earn-Money

Bushnell, M. B. (2021, February 3). *The 7 Best Finance Books for Teens in 2021*. Investopedia.Com. https://www.investopedia.com/best-finance-books-for-teens-5095590

Carrns, A. C. (2018, August 24). *Retirement Planning in High School? It's Never Too Early, Experts Say*. Nytimes.Com. https://www.nytimes.com/2018/08/24/your-money/roth-ira-retirement-teenagers.html

Charles Schwab. (2021, February 26). *Saving for College: Custodial Accounts.* Schwab.Com. https://www.schwab. com/resource-center/insights/content/saving-for-college-custodial-accounts

Creel, S. C. (2020, June 3). *Five Tips for Teaching Kids Empathy + Evidence-Based Activities.* Undefiningmother-hood.Com. https://tinyurl.com/2p8mtkvz

Doyle, A. D. (2019, August 12). *First Job Ideas for Teens.* Thebalancecareers.Com. https://www.thebalancecareers. com/list-of-good-first-job-ideas-for-teens-2062235

DuPaix, M. D. (2019, November 20). *Good Jobs for Teenagers.* Thebalanceeveryday.Com. https://www. thebalanceeveryday.com/jobs-for-teenagers-2085438

Hayes, D. H. (2021, March 8). *28 Passive Income Ideas That Actually Work.* Wellkeptwallet.Com. https:// wellkeptwallet.com/passive-income-ideas/

Jacob, J. (2020, May 24). *Spreadsheet for Budgeting Monthly in 2021.* Teenfinancialfreedom.Com. https:// teenfinancialfreedom.com/spreadsheet-for-budgeting-monthly/

Kerry, K. (n.d.). *Age-Appropriate Chores for Kids – Lists by Developmental Stage.* Selfsufficientkids.Com. Retrieved February 27, 2021, from https://selfsufficientkids.com/age-appropriate-chores-for-kids/

LaScala, M. L. (2020, June 1). *The Best Chores for Kids Teach Them Helping out Is Part of Being a Family*. Goodhousekeeping.Com. https://www.goodhousekeeping.com/life/parenting/a32702630/best-chores-for-kids/

Maranjian, S. M. (2018, July 10). *Compound Interest and Compounding Growth: A Comprehensive Guide*. Fool.Com. https://www.fool.com/retirement/2018/07/10/compound-interest-and-compounding-growth-a-compreh.aspx

McClanahan, A. M. (2018, December 27). *19 Streams of Income You Can Launch Right Now*. Principlesofincrease.Com. https://principlesofincrease.com/streams-of-income/

Monster. (n.d.). *10 Questions to Ask People at the Top of Their Game*. Monster.Com. Retrieved March 13, 2021, from https://www.monster.com/career-advice/article/questions-to-ask-successful-people

Morin, A. M. (2021, February 16). *Chores List for Older Kids and Teens*. Verywellfamily.Com. https://www.verywellfamily.com/over-50-ideas-of-chores-for-teens-2609291

Ramsey Solutions. (2020, August 7). *Why Your Kids Don't Need an Allowance*. Daveramsey.Com. https://www.daveramsey.com/blog/why-kids-shouldnt-get-an-allowance

Royal, J. R. (2021, March 4). *14 passive income ideas to help you make money in 2021*. Bankrate.Com. https://tinyurl.com/2p92vkaw

Schwab. (n.d.). *What are the Benefits of a Schwab One Custodial Account?* Schwab.Com. Retrieved March 5, 2021, from https://tinyurl.com/5n857nc2

Singh, B. S. (2018, January 5). *Is the development of your child on track? Know here!* Studmonkedtech.Com. http://studmonkedtech.com/blog/know-early-childhood-developmental-milestones/

Team The WisdomPost and Sophia. (n.d.). *Billionaires And Their Reading Habits*. Thewisdompost.Com. Retrieved February 13, 2021, from https://www.thewisdompost.com/reading/billionaires-and-their-reading-habits/1073

Wells Fargo Bank. (n.d.). *Kids Savings Account*. Wellsfargo.-Com. Retrieved February 27, 2021, from https://www.wellsfargo.com/savings-cds/kids

Wright, K. W. (2020, March 19). *All the chores your kids should be doing, based on their age*. Reviewed.Com. https://www.reviewed.com/parenting/features/age-appropriate-chores-for-children-chore-lists-for-kids-of-every-age